LOVE

and all the other verbs of Life

LOVE
and all the other verbs of Life

by

Peter McWilliams

Doubleday & Company, Inc.

Garden City, New York   1973

ISBN: 0-385-02116-X
Library of Congress Catalog Card Number 72–92229
Copyright © 1973 by Peter McWilliams
PRINTED IN THE UNITED STATES OF AMERICA
FIRST EDITION

CONTENTS

ONE OUCH: LOVE 1

TWO NO MORE 13

THREE KEEP RISTMA IN CHRISTMAS 19

FOUR GREETINGS 35

FIVE BLOOM FOR ME 39

SIX THE SMILE OF GOD 55

SEVEN I CAN'T GO 75

EIGHT SO HERE I AM AGAIN 81

NINE A FEW THINGS YOU LEFT BEHIND
YOU'LL NEVER MISS: 101

ONE

OUCH: LOVE

I have been
free
now for
quite some time.

free
from the idea
that I needed
any one one
to share with me
the limits of my
existence.

but now
you've
come along,
and I find
the lack of
you
turns my
alone
moments into
lonely ones.

ouch:
love.

HELLO HALLMARK,
GOODBYE FRANCE

or

WHEN YOU DARE
ENOUGH TO SEND THE
VERY VERSED

Open your mind
and you will find
A person there
that needs to care.

And when your person
feels alone,
Remember, mine is
always home.

I wanted to
spend the night with you
eat with you
take you to meet my friends
make you one of them
take you to bed
make you one with me
say I love you
hear you say the same
meditate, with your heartbeat as my mantra.

I wanted the sun,
and a goodly portion of the moon.

All I got was this poem,
which I wanted to be
a happy one.

of course
you said you'd call.

of course
I waited all day for
The Call.

of course
it never came.

It's just too late
I'm in too deep.
I think you're great
I cannot sleep.

I got those
I-need-you-you-don't-need-me-
I-gotta-make-you-want-me-baby
blues.

The January bee is cool.
The February bee is fine.
The March bee is all right.
The April bee is OK.
But that Maybe I can't stand.

yes
or
no
.

"maybe" is no.
"I'm not sure" is no.
"I need more time" is no.
"yes or no what?" is DEFINITELY no!

only yes is yes.
anything else is no.

and why should I be hurt?
it was just a weekend thing.
right?

we didn't speak of love.
we hardly spoke at all.

just stared at each other.
and touched without fear.

I was uncomfortable
in all that comfort.

but you're home now.
and so am I.

home to pain, where I live;

except on exceptional
weekends.

it's all right.

I'll mend.

I mean,
I guess I'll mend.

I mean,
I always have

I didn't need
a lot
of love.

only a little.

enough to see if
It still existed.

to see if
I still existed.

thanks anyway
for your time.

TWO

NO MORE

I am not ready to give love.

not really.

I offer it often enough,
but only to those who
have neither the
desire nor capacity
to receive.

waste.
self-deceit.

(more)

those persons who
can and will
take my love,
who appreciate it,
savor it,
and return a goodly measure
of their own
scare the shit out of me.

I tremble.

if these words were printed
in my hand and not passed through
several typesetting machines
before your reading,
you could see the tremors—
the shaking lettering.

I give these god-creatures
of my existence subsistence
portions of love. rations.
token gestures of affection.
questionable comfort.
68 degree warmth.

(more, more)

yet to the dum-dums,
the fear caged carcasses,
the mobile zombies,
the selfless non-centered
defense dealers

I give my all.

plus what I can
beg, borrow, and especially steal.

(no more)

THREE

KEEP RISTMA IN CHRISTMAS

I'm not quite
as certain of
my uncertainties.

I am beginning to
doubt my doubts.

And I'm having
second thoughts
about my
second thoughts.

I appreciate solitude.
I romanticize it sometimes.

Some growth has taken place.
I haven't taken time to
notice.

I sat
evaluating
myself.

I decided
to lie down.

does the sogginess of a need
evaporate into clouds that
are destined to reign again
?

a lone
a love

they look alike,
but there any resemblance
ends.

I don't need some
one
to be my joy.

I do need
someone
to share
my joys with.

friendship
is the
University
of the
Universe.

I
am
a
plum

fast
becoming
a
prune.

ingesting my joys,
my needs exhale pain,
intensifying my
emotional pollution.

If only I knew
someone
as well as I knew
my loneliness.

I wonder what
all the other
lonely people
of the world
are doing
tonight.

LIFE:

loving
healing   losing
hurting

keep
ristma
in
Christmas.

I
need
some
one
to
sing
my
self
to

FOUR

GREETINGS

hellohellohellohellohellohellohellohellohellohellohellohellohellohello

hellohellohellohellohellohellohellohello hellohellohellohellohellohell

FIVE

BLOOM FOR ME

nothing
is quite
as exciting
as meeting*
a new person
and discovering*
a new me.

[*interchangeable]

after searching
so hard for
so long
I was sure to find
something.

thank God
it was you.

be careful.

I will
end it
if it goes even
slightly wrong.

I am worn from suffering.

the prospect of pleasure
will not motivate me
through pain
for long.

at least not now.

be full. care.

please.

what should I do about you.
about my feelings about you.
about my feelings about me about you.

for you,
are we

something to

kill time with
or
make time for?

if you
hurt me
I'll take the pain,

but I'll never
be open to you
again.

what's going on
in your mind

would help me know

what's going on
in mine.

I'm glad you can cry.
I'm glad you can come over
and put your head in my lap
and cry. I'm glad you can
say "I guess I don't like
myself very much." I'm
glad you can.

I never could.

is it my
perception
or my
projection
that makes
me think
you
like me
too.

your feeling about

what is
going on

is more important than

what is
going on

I am adaptable.
I can play any game
any way you like.
Or, maybe, I can
give up games entirely,
for a while,
if that's what you want.

I want you,
and I'm willing to
change the external
me to get you
(it's changing all the time anyway).

The internal me is
a glow right now.
Of love and need.

I glow well for you.

how much
I want
to hear
you say
the words
I want
to say
to you.

want me

as much as I

need you

bloom
for
me

SIX

THE SMILE OF GOD

love is a
jungle of
beasts.

love is a
garden of
flowers.

love is a
question.

love is the
answer.

love is
complex.

love is
simple.

love is
pain.

love is
joy.

I have
no one
to love.

I have.

you make
flowers
of my
hours.

today
was a
bouquet.

I fall in love
a thousand times
with each new you
I find.

I need you
like a
hole in the head.

like the hole in the head
I breathe from.

I have taken these few minutes
away from us
to write about you.

Love.

I have filled how many pages
with love verse . . . dare I say
that this is the first time
I have loved?

with you I dare anything.
for you I care everything.

my joy knows no words.

I love . . .
and
oh.

oh oh oh oh
oh oh oh oh oh oh oh
ohoh
oh oh oh oh oh oh oh oh
oh
oh oh oh
ohohohohohohohohohho
hohohohohohohohohohohohoho
hohohohoho
ho ho ho ho ho ho
ho ho ho ho
ho

with you I am so
whole
that I don't even
need sex,

although I am not
totally opposed
to the notion

HAIKU YOU

the morning dew
and me and you
at last together
in this haiku.

one
touch
is worth
ten thousand
words.

I'd follow you
to the ends
of the bed.

I Love You.

some of the hardest words
in the world to say.

some of the
hardest
not to.

I need
no more
than
you

and
what
ever
it is
we do

at a point
somewhere between
atomic fission and
the smile of God
lies my love for
you.

lovers
discovered electricity
long before
Benjamin Franklin
was told to
go fly a kite.

will this never end?

I am not concerned.

it has lasted
forever already.

you must never leave me.
if you leave me you must never return.
if you ever return you must never leave me again.

of you
only God
cares more
than I

SEVEN

I CAN'T GO

I'm tired of running
from me
and I'm scared of
discovering what's
there . . . er . . . here.

and I'm
alienated
and
lonely
to the point of
paralysis.

so here I sit and write.
and there you sit and read.

I can go
days, weeks, months, years
without you.

—but
never to see you again.

I can't go.

I don't care.

Yes I do.

I only wish
I didn't care.

good
god
go

EIGHT

SO HERE I AM AGAIN

so here I am.

desperately waving my arms.
trying to keep whatever
balance I have left.
waiting to see my life
flash by before I hit
bottom
        again.

I felt
I needed you.

I was right

I treated you
not quite as good as I could.

I was left

I thought
I wouldn't miss you much.

I was wrong

It's not really
you
I miss.

It's what I
let myself
feel & be & do
while you're near.

A "COME HOME, COME BACK" POEM:

please.

god! I loved you.

more than
either of us
realized
at the time.

I found
in you
a home.

Your departure
left me a
shelterless victim
of a
major disaster.

I called the
Red Cross,
but they wouldn't
send over
a nurse.

I gradually
withdrew
from
everything
you ever
touched.

my body,
the bed,
shoes,
chairs,
mirrors,
records,
books,

my mind.

YOULE

My mind and body weakened
by a common cold.

My mother said I was taking
so much vitamin C I would
turn into an orange. The only
thing I've turned into so
far is a methane factory.

It is Christmas eve.

I pity me, curse my isolation,
and hate you that I cannot
love you any more.

I was almost well.

Two months and three days ago
California called. And you
answered.

God, wish your Son a
happy birthday.

St. Nick, grant me one gift:

no more memories of what
might have been
until my cold
has melted.

I am missing you
far better than
I ever loved you.

Where does it go
when it dies?

Love, I mean.

Does it go to some
heavenly common
burial ground,

or to an individual
plot on the graver
half of each man's
heart.

Wherever it may be,
I would like to visit there,

bring some flowers,
and lay Us to rest.

This is the only
thing
you ever gave me,

a new english translation of
The Bible.

The only physical relic
of our relationship.

This bible is becoming
        Holy.

I heard you were in
Florida with
what's-his-name
with the hairy back.

that bastard.

always trying to get
at
you while we were together.

he no doubt drove out to
California, swept you in his
arms (you always were fond of
dramatics), tied you to the
hood of his Volkswagen (he
always did call you "dear"),
and drove you off to the land
of the setting sun.

I hope you've found your little
splot of paradise
with what's-his-name
with the hairy back.

life is becoming
less livable.

with each new person I meet
I wonder, is this the day
fate has chosen, or is fate
what I have chosen to get me
through the day.

loving
is the most
creative
force of the universe.

the memory of loving
the most
destructive.

I am lonely.
I am dying.
I fall to the
ground crying.

people gather
in a circle
around me.

one throws me
a pen. another
a piece of paper.

"Here.
Write a poem about
what you feel. We
will tell you how
good it is, how
well we relate to
it, and you will
feel better."

will I never
lose this loss?

will I never say

"yes.

I am
free

I am
me."

and laugh.

and mean it.

In your
mad dash
to be
free,

you lost a
freedom.

you are
not free
to return.

one thing I forgot:

after the
pain of parting
comes the
happiness of healing.

rediscovering
   life,
   friends,
   my self.

Joy.

the blossom
is brown and
dead.

the seeds are looking
for some new ground
to grow.

---

NINE

*A FEW THINGS
YOU LEFT BEHIND
YOU'LL NEVER MISS:*

one suitcase, empty.

one paperback, bookmark on page 113.

two socks, one white one black.

one tennis shoe, left.

one record, scratched.

me.

brush; plastic handle, nylon bristles.

one key, lock unknown.

one love poem, incomplete.